FREE Gift fro[illegible]rtie

~~~

As a special thank you for owning this book
Bertie will send a personalised FREE Gift 😊

CLICK HERE to get your FREE Gift

http://BertieBrachiosaurus.com
~~~

Bertie Santasaurus

Bertie Santasaurus

By Ash Azalea

Illustrated by Lucy Beach

Copyright

Bertie Santasaurus ©

By Ash Azalea

Bertie Brachiosaurus Dinosaur Adventures Series
Edition 2

ISBN: 978-1-9164220-2-5

Dedicated to Filomena who inspires with love & kindness always.

Phlumf!

"Hey!" I shout as a dinosaur-size snowball lands on my head and knocks me into the deep snow.

"Got you back, he he" bellows Bertie Brachiosaurus to the delight of my friends whose laughter is shortened as each of them is quickly flattened by a Bertie snowball.

"I'm loving this snowball game" laughs Bertie as a flurry of snowballs lands on him from me and my friends.

"Bye Lucy, Aiden, Sally. Happy Christmas!" I say grabbing the sledge ready for the journey home.

"Happy Christmas Astin; Happy Christmas Bertie" shout back my friends.

"OK let's go home and hang-up our stockings" I say.

Bertie and I jump on the sledge and whizz down a big hill.

"Wheee" I squeal excitedly

"This is such fun!" shouts Bertie

There is a sharp bend at the bottom of the hill. I get the turn wrong and we crash into a tree stump. The sledge breaks and we fly through the air.

"Whoaaaaa"

...and land in a big snowdrift,

Our heads pop out of the snow facing each other. "Oh no. Now we will have to walk home, and we'll be late for supper. Dad will be cross." I say. But Bertie isn't listening; his eyes wide open he is pointing to something behind me.

"Santa Claus!" I gasp.

"Ho, ho ho. I thought I was the only one who can fly" chuckles Santa Claus. "You two have caught me by surprise, I don't usually let children see me on Christmas Eve."

"We are so happy to see you Santa. I'm Astin and this is Bertie Brachiosaurus" I say with a huge smile on my face.

Santa's smile fades as he explains that he was doing the first Christmas delivery for all the small children who have already gone to bed when he had a bad landing and two of his reindeer got injured. Now he was delayed as he is waiting for the replacement reindeer to fly in from the North Pole.

"I'm worried that all the children may not get their presents in time for when they wake up on Christmas Day." He says sadly.

Then I have an idea. “Maybe Bertie could pull the sleigh? He’s very strong.”

“That is very kind of you.” says Santa, his smile returning. “That would really help!”

Bertie is so excited to be pulling the sleigh and really happy to help the little children get their presents delivered on time.

“We must be very quiet” says Santa “so that none of the towns folk see us”

He gives Bertie a special pair of reindeer antlers to wear, he looks so funny.

Bertie is really enjoying pulling the sleigh as he slides down the lanes. He is as excited as I am to have met Santa.

The sleigh is surprisingly warm! Maybe Santa has seat heaters haha

We whizz around a bend in the road and suddenly I see some figures ahead.

"Oh no! It's my friends, Lucy, Sally & Aiden!" I exclaim. "What if they see us?"

Now I am really worried as I know Santa really should not be seen by anyone on Christmas Eve. I know Bertie and I have seen him, but we are helping in a Santa Emergency.

"HoHoHo. No problem Astin" says Santa as he pulls out his phone and sends a text.

Suddenly a snowstorm surrounds us.

"What did you do Santa?" I ask.

"I sent a message to my good friend the Snow Queen asking her to send Jack Frost, the cheeky little imp, to give us a snowstorm as cover. HoHoHo" laughs Santa.

"I just thought, Bertie cannot fly. How will you get in the houses?" I ask

"Ho, ho. I may be old, but you will be surprised how high I can jump, after all I've been doing it for many years." laughs Santa.

When we stop at the first house, Santa Claus takes a hop and a jump and then he is on top of the roof and popping down the chimney with his sack of presents.

Bertie is so fast as we race from house to house. Santa is amazed at his strength and speed.

"Bertie, I think I'm going to call you 'Bertie *Santasaurus*' " chuckles Santa Claus.

“Bertie is awesome! I’ve made-up the time I lost already. Now all the children will get their presents in time for Christmas Day.” Says Santa, feeling really happy.

We finish delivering around the town and return to the clearing in the wood where the new reindeer have arrived. We tether them to the sleigh ready to fly around the world from Australia, through Asia and Europe to Canada and the USA.

Santa and I feed the injured reindeer some special Christmas snacks. “You all rest in the wood until you feel ready to return to the North Pole” Santa tells them.

“Right Bertie & Astin I must give you a lift home, jump aboard.” Instructs Santa.

And this time we really do fly.

“Wow!” I squeal

“Wohooooo, this is even better than sledging!” shouts an excited Bertie as we fly above the rooftops of friends’ houses before landing in the garden at home.

"Wow, we've got home on time. Santa's sleigh is a great way to travel" I exclaim.

"Bertie and Astin, you have helped to make sure children all across the world will get their presents delivered on time; thank you so much." And then Santa sticks 'Santa's Official Helper' badges on us.

"Remember, you need to be asleep if Santa is going to visit your bedroom tonight!

Merry Christmas! Ho Ho Ho"

"How was the sledging?" Asks Mum cheerily.

"Great! And we helped Santa!" I say in a rush.

"Haha Great imagination as always Astin." laughs Uncle Tim.

"Time for bed." says Dad. "You know Santa will only visit once everyone is asleep"

It's Christmas Day!

"Nice sledge Astin and great antlers Bertie!" Says Dad.

I don't' remember getting those? Quizzes Mum

"And it says to *Bertie Santasaurus* on the label!" chuckles Uncle Tim.

Merry Christmas everyone!

Merry Christmas!

THE END

Also available:

Bertie Brachiosaurus

~~~

Coming Soon:

...

Bertie Brachiosaurus Colouring Book

...

Bertie Brachiosaurus Kid's Diary Journal

...

Follow Bertie on Facebook:

facebook.com/BertieBrachiosaurus
~~~

Ash Azalea

Ash Azalea has enjoyed an eclectic life and global travel. Four children have helped maintain a youthful mindset, inspiring the idea and encouraging the creation of the character, Bertie Brachiosaurus.

Lucy Beach

Lucy Beach is a country girl at heart who loves animals, horse-riding, gardening & nature. A world away, she also has a deep interest in the Korean language & culture. Having studied Illustration at University, Bertie Santasaurus is her third children's book.

~~~

FREE Gift from Bertie

~~~

As a special thank you for owning this book Bertie will send a personalised FREE Gift 😊

CLICK HERE to get your FREE Gift

http://BertieBrachiosaurus.com

Printed in Great Britain
by Amazon

71771633R00022